Flamboyance

AND OTHER EXTRAVAGANCES OF GOD ON DISPLAY

Joan Wood
Illustrated by: Juliana Fulton

Flamboyance

Extravagances of God on display

All Scripture is taken from the following versions: NKJV, NIV, NLT, & NASB.

@ 2025 by Joan Wood

Author: Joan Wood

Illustrator: Juliana Fulton

Publisher: 5 Stones Publishing

Publication Date: June 2025

ISBN: 978-1-945423-69-7

This book is dedicated to my one and only Chris Wood, our amazing family, Matt, Mary, Hudson & Otis. Ben, Sarah, Isabelle & Joshua. David, Anna, Johanna, Lydia, Emma & Amelia. And to my family and friends who love me and let me be the best version of Jesus I can be!

Table of Contents

Introduction

I am fascinated with God.

Psalm 145:3 *"Great is the Lord, and greatly to be praised. His greatness is unsearchable."*

This little book was written with a couple of intentions.

First, my purpose is that we would have some "awe" moments with our amazing God. God has so many mysteries, and yet He loves to reveal Himself to us so that we can know Him more. He displays His greatness throughout creation and mankind. Every time I see the myriad of colors in a peacock's feathers, touch the wrinkled, yet sensitive skin of an elephant, or hear the distinct calls of friendly dolphins, I am astounded by God's immense creativity. He does these incredible things just because He can!

Secondly, for fun! Whether leading or being a member of many mission teams around the world, I try to bring an element of fun. I think Jesus enjoyed the people He was with and had happy times of merriment and laughter. I compiled these fun facts for others to use while traveling together as entertaining readings with thoughtful questions for honest reflection and team building.

Just for fun: Before you read the Bible verses, ask others for suggestions. See how many different Bible verses can be applied to each fun fact and drop me a note...Maybe we'll compile book 2 together! ☺

Joan

Flamboyance

Fun Fact

- A group of flamingos is called a flamboyance.
- The definition of flamboyance is the tendency to attract attention because of one's exuberance, confidence, and stylishness.

Thought

- When the Body of Christ comes together, the glory of God is displayed.

Bible

- Psalm 133:1 " *Behold, How good and how pleasant it is for brethren to dwell together in unity.*"
- Romans 12:5 "*So we, being many, are one body in Christ, and individually members of one another.*"
- Romans 15:7 "*Therefore receive one another, just as Christ also received us, to the glory of God.*"
- John 13:35 "*By this all will know that you are My disciples, if you have love for one another.*"

Discussion

- In what ways can we come together as the Body of Christ?
- What keeps us from coming together as the Body of Christ?
- Who can you display the glory of God with today?

Names & Nicknames

Fun Fact

- Dolphins have names for each other. They have a signature whistle to identify themselves and use these whistles to call to one another.

Thought

- Names are important. Jesus called Peter by a new name, denoting his destiny in God. Names and nicknames can be a form of encouragement and edification.

Bible

- Matthew 16:18 *" Now I say to you that you are Peter (which means rock), and upon this rock I will build my church, and all the powers of hell will not conquer it."*
- Acts 4:36 *"For instance, there was Joseph, the one the apostles nicknamed Barnabas* (which means 'son of encouragement')."
- Mark 3:17 *"James and John (the sons of Zebedee, but Jesus nicknamed them 'Sons of Thunder')."*

Discussion

- Who can you encourage today with a new nickname? Maybe the person next to you?
- What's your nickname? Radiant? Cheerful? Generous?
- John (one of the sons of thunder) had his name changed again to "beloved one". What changed?
- Maybe you've been thought of in a not-so-glorious way. Is it possible to change? How?

Pineapples

Fun Fact

- It takes about 2 years for a single pineapple to grow before it can be harvested.

Thought

- Keep on growing in the Lord. Your perserverance will be rewarded!

Bible

- Luke 2:52 *"Jesus grew in wisdom and in stature and in favor with God and all the people."*

- I Samuel 2:26 *"And the boy Samuel continued to grow in stature and in favor with the Lord and with people."*

- 2 Peter 1:5-7 *"But also for this very reason, giving all diligence, add to your faith virtue, to virtue knowledge, to knowledge self-control, to self-control perseverance, to perseverance godliness, to godliness brotherly kindness, and to brotherly kindness love."*

- Psalm 92:12 *"The righteous will flourish like a palm tree; they will grow like a cedar of Lebanon."*

Discussion

- What does it mean to you to grow in the Lord?
- When do you grow the most, in good times or hard times? Share your thoughts about that.
- When pineapples grow, they need tending. What would that look like in your life as you grow?
- What does the fruit taste like if it's not fully grown?

Endless Eyesight

Fun Fact

- The eyes can distinguish approximately 10 million colors and process images faster than the most advanced computer.
- Camels have 3 eyelids to protect their eyes.

Thought

- Guard your eyes, be aware of what you look at, and let in.

Bible

- Psalm 26:3 *"For Your lovingkindness is before my eyes, and I have walked in Your truth."*
- Psalm 101:3 *"I will set nothing wicked before my eyes."*
- Psalm 123:1 *"Unto You I lift my eyes, O You who dwell in the heavens."*
- Revelation 5:11,12 *"Then I looked, and I heard the voice of many angels around the throne, the living creatures, and the elders; and the number of them was ten thousand times ten thousand, and thousands of thousands, saying with a loud voice: "Worthy is the Lamb who was slain to receive power and riches and wisdom and strength and honor and glory and blessing!"*

Discussion

- How easy is it to forget something you've seen?
- What are some ways you can put a guard around your eyes?
- Read Revelation 4 and see all the colors describing heaven and heavenly things.

Ice Cream Cones

Fun Fact

- The ice cream cone was invented at the World's Fair in St Louis in 1904 when an ice cream vendor ran out of bowls, and a nearby waffle maker saved the day.

Thought

- You may be the solution to someone else's problem.

Bible

- Ecclesiastes 4:9 *"Two are better than one because they have a good reward for their labor."*

- I Corinthians 12:12 *"Just as a body, though one, has many parts, but all its many parts form one body, so it is with Christ."*

- Philippians 2:1-4 *"Is there any encouragement from belonging to Christ? Any comfort from his love? Any fellowship together in the Spirit? Are your hearts tender and compassionate? ² Then make me truly happy by agreeing wholeheartedly with each other, loving one another, and working together with one mind and purpose. ³ Don't be selfish; don't try to impress others. Be humble, thinking of others as better than yourselves. ⁴ Don't look out only for your own interests, but take an interest in others, too."*

Discussion

- How can you help someone today?
- Are you aware of others' needs around you?
- What is one gift/talent that the Lord has given you that might blend with someone else?

Arctic Tern

Fun Fact

- The Arctic Tern holds the record for the longest migratory journey of any bird, up to 59,000 miles round-trip between its breeding grounds and wintering grounds.

Thought

- You may feel lonely or like you're a long way from home, but God always knows where you are.

Bible

- Matthew 10:29-31 *"What is the price of two sparrows– one copper coin? But not a single sparrow can fall to the ground without your Father knowing it. And the very hairs of your head are all numbered. So don't be afraid; you are more valuable to God than a whole flock of sparrows."*

- Deuteronomy 31:8 *"And the Lord, He is the One who goes before you. He will be with you; He will not leave you nor forsake you; do not fear nor be dismayed."*

- 1 Corinthians 15:58 *"Therefore, my beloved, be steadfast, immovable, always abounding in the work of the Lord, knowing your labor is not in vain in the Lord."*

Discussion

- What are some things you can do to stay focused on your present mission?
- How can you encourage yourself in the Lord?
- What about asking someone to pray with you?

Companion Cows

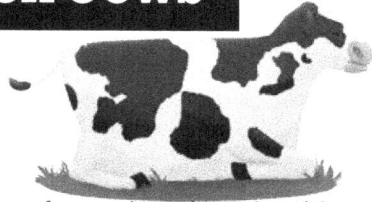

Fun Fact

- Cows have best friends. Cows form close bonds with other cows and often have best friends within their herds. These social animals can become stressed when separated from their companions.

Thought

- To have a friend, you must be a friend.

- One of the greatest treasures in the Kingdom of God is friendship. How we treat and serve one another displays the gift of friendship!

Bible

- Proverbs 18:24 *"A man who has friends must himself be friendly, But there is a friend who sticks closer than a brother."*

- John 15:13 *"Greater love has no one than this, than to lay down one's life for his friends."*

Discussion

- What does it mean to be a friend?
- How can you be a better friend to someone?
- Who are your friends?
- What's the difference between a friend and an acquaintance?
- How do we love others selflessly unless we have God's love powering that love?

Brimming Brains

Fun Fact

- Your brain is learning throughout your entire lifetime. The brain's neuroplasticity allows it to rewire and adapt throughout life in response to learning and experiences.

Thought

- You can train your brain!

Bible

- Philippians 4:8 *"And now, dear brothers and sisters, one final thing. Fix your thoughts on what is true, and honorable, and right, and pure, and lovely, and admirable. Think about things that are excellent and worthy of praise."*

- Romans 12:2 *"And do not be conformed to this world, but be transformed by the renewing of your mind, that you may prove what is that good and acceptable and perfect will of God."*

- Ephesians 1:17-19 *"The glorious Father, may give you the Spirit of wisdom and revelation, so that you may know him better. 18 I pray that the eyes of your heart may be enlightened so that you may know the hope to which he has called you."*

Discussion

- What are some ways you can train your brain?
- Which of your experiences affect the way your brain thinks?
- Everyone has patterns of thinking. Does yours need to be adjusted?
- Identify negative thought patterns and apply the Word of God to them to change them...It's possible!

Terrific Teeth

Fun Fact

- Dogs have 28 baby teeth and 42 permanent teeth. Cats have 26 baby teeth and 30 permanent teeth and can't move their jaws sideways. Snails can have 1,000–12,000 teeth. Mosquitoes have 47 teeth. Humans have 20 baby teeth and 32 permanent teeth.

Thought

- God has created us uniquely.

Bible

- Psalm 139:14 "*I praise you because I am fearfully and wonderfully made; your works are wonderful; I know that full well.*"
- Genesis 1:27 "*So God created human beings in his own image. In the image of God, he created them; male and female, he created them.*"

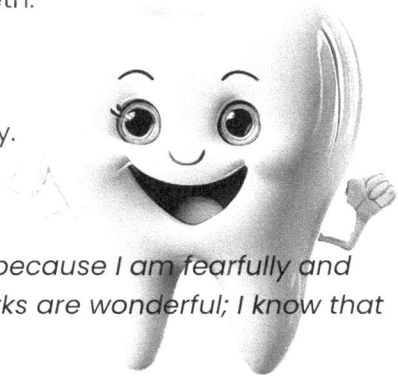

Discussion

- In what other ways can you see God's hand in creating you and me?
- In what ways are you unique?
- What other "teeth" references in the Bible can you think of?
  - Gnashing teeth: Matthew 22:13
  - White teeth: Genesis 49:12
  - By the skin of my teeth: Job 19:20

Sunny Smiles

Fun Fact

- Smiling can boost your mood, even if it's forced. The act of smiling triggers the release of dopamine. Dopamine is a chemical messenger in the brain that influences motivation and pleasure.

Thought

- A Smile changes everything, even you!   Even when you don't feel happy, smile! It will help change your mood. Smiling welcomes others to smile too! Smiling is contagious!

Bible

- Psalm 146:5 *"Happy is he who has the God of Jacob for his help, whose hope is in the Lord his God."*
- Proverbs 15:13 *"A glad heart makes a happy face; a broken heart crushes the spirit".*

Discussion

- Have you ever tried 20 forced smiles in a row? Try It!
- Who can you give the gift of a smile to today?
- Experiment: Smile at everyone you see and count how many smile back at you.

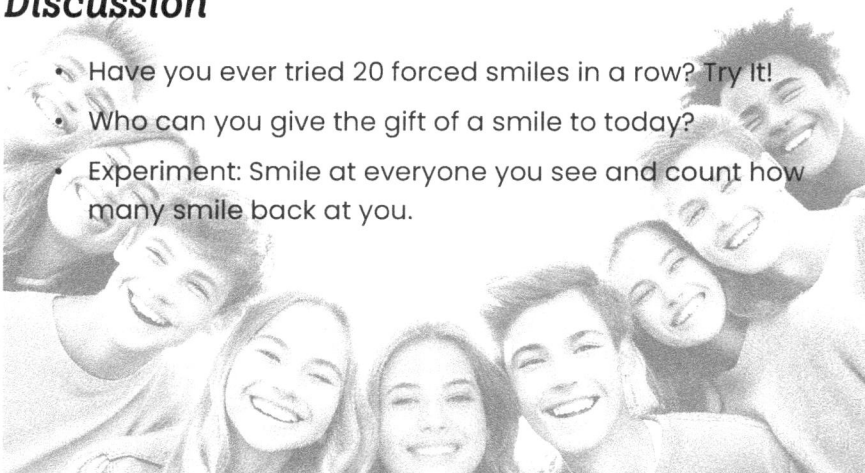

Attention Span

Fun Fact

- Studies suggest that the average attention span of a human is now shorter than that of a goldfish, lasting around 9 seconds.

Thought

- Do you have trouble listening to someone for more than a few minutes? To improve your attention span, eliminate distractions, and do activities that require sustained attention, like reading. Stop multitasking and quiet yourself.

Bible

- Joshua 1:8 *"Study this book of instruction continually. Meditate on it day and night so you will be sure to obey everything written in it., Only then will you prosper and succeed in all you do."*
- Psalm 46:10 *"Be still and know that I am God."*
- Psalm 27:4 *"One thing I ask from the Lord, this only do I seek: that I may dwell in the house of the Lord all the days of my life, to gaze on the beauty of the Lord and to seek him in his temple."*

Discussion

- What helps you pay attention?
- What are some things you can do to increase your attention span?
- What does it mean to practice stillness? Quiet?
- How does the concept of "one thing" help you focus?

Countless Cells

Fun Fact

- The human body has approximately 37.2 trillion cells, each with a specific role in maintaining health.

Thought

- We are the Body of Christ, and each has a specific role in maintaining the health of His body, the Church.

Bible

- 1 Corinthians 12:4-7 *"There are different kinds of spiritual gifts, but the same Spirit is the source of them all. [5] There are different kinds of service, but we serve the same Lord. [6] God works in different ways, but it is the same God who does the work in all of us. [7] A spiritual gift is given to each of us so we can help each other."*

- Romans 12:7 *"If your gift is serving others, serve them well. If you are a teacher, teach well."*

Discussion

- What specific gifts and talents do you have to benefit the Body of Christ?
- How do you use them to benefit the Body of Christ?
- Are there any that you are not currently using?
- How does this affect the Body of Christ?

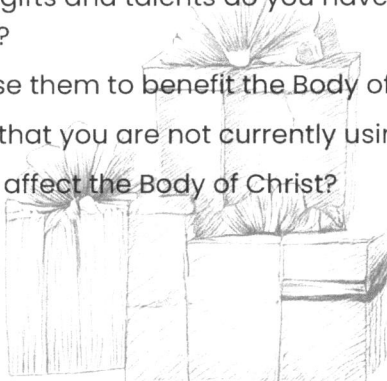

The Tiniest Bone

Fun Fact

- The stapes bone in the human ear is the smallest bone in the body, but it plays a crucial role in hearing.

Thought

- Hearing is crucial to following the Lord.

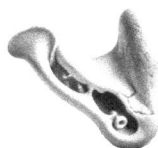

Bible

- Romans 10:17 *"So then faith comes by hearing, and hearing by the Word of God"*
- John 10:27 *"My sheep hear My voice, and I know them, and they follow Me."*
- Proverbs 4:10 *"Hear, my son, and receive my sayings. And the years of your life will be many."*
- Matthew 7:24 *"Therefore, whoever hears these sayings of Mine, and does them, I will liken him to a wise man who built his house on the rock."*
- Deuteronomy 4:6 *"Hear O Israel, The Lord our God, the Lord is One!"*
- Proverbs 2:2 *"Incline your ear to wisdom and apply your heart to understanding."*

Discussion

- How important is hearing and acting on what you hear?
- What can you do to hear God's voice more clearly?
- When you hear God's voice, how quickly do you respond?

Jumping Fleas

Fun Fact

- Fleas can jump 350 times their body length.

Thought

- God can do exceedingly more than we can think or imagine!

Bible

- Matthew 19:26 *"Jesus looked at them and said to them," With men this is impossible, but with God all things are possible."*

- Ephesians 3:20 *"Now to Him who is able to do exceedingly, abundantly above all that we ask or think, according to the power that works in us..."*

Discussion

- Is there anything you are facing right now that seems impossible? If so, remind yourself of who God is!

- Pause and think: Is there anything that God cannot do?

Your Nose Knows

Fun Fact

- Human noses can distinguish between scents, in fact, around 1 trillion different scents, showcasing their remarkable olfactory abilities.
- A dog's sense of smell is 1000 times greater than a human's and is commonly used to guide and direct.
- Slugs have 4 noses.

Thought

- As sensitive as our noses are, and are beneficial to our well-being, how much more valuable is it that our spirit is sensitive to the Holy Spirit, and His guidance in our lives?

Bible

- John 14:26 *"But the Helper, the Holy Spirit, whom the Father will send in My name, He will teach you all things and bring to your remembrance all things that I said to you."*
- Psalm 51:11 *"Do not cast me away from Your presence, and do not take Your Holy Spirit from me."*
- Luke 4:1 *"Then Jesus, being filled with the Holy Spirit, returned from the Jordan and was led by the Spirit into the wilderness."*

Discussion

- How does the Holy Spirit lead and guide you?
- How can you stay sensitive to the Holy Spirit?
- Share a life story of when you felt you were led by the Holy Spirit.

Tame-able Tongue

Fun Fact

- The blue whale is the largest animal on Earth, and its tongue can weigh as much as an adult elephant, between 4000 and 8000 lbs.
- The human tongue is composed of eight muscles, making it the strongest muscle in the body.
- The average tongue is about 3 inches long and 1.5 inches wide.
- Just like fingerprints, every tongue is unique in its shape, size, and taste bud distribution.
- Your tongue can say over 90 words in a minute.
- Tongue Health Reflects Overall Health: The appearance and condition of the tongue can indicate overall health issues, such as vitamin deficiencies or infections.
- Crocodiles can't stick their tongues out.

Thought

- Have you ever heard the saying "See no evil, hear no evil, speak no evil"? Our tongues can bring smiles and bless people, or the opposite.
- Words can be used to launch others into their destiny.

Bible

- James 3:4 *"Look also at ships: although they are so large and are driven by fierce winds, they are turned by a very small rudder wherever the pilot desires. 5 Even so the tongue is a little member and boasts great things"*
- James 3:8 *"But no man can tame the tongue. It is an unruly evil, full of deadly poison."*

- James 3:10 *"Out of the same mouth proceed blessing and cursing. My brethren, these things ought not to be so."*
- John 6:63 *"It is the Spirit who gives life; the flesh profits nothing. The words that I speak to you are spirit, and they are life."*
- 1 Peter 3:10 *"For He who would love life and see good days, let him refrain his tongue from evil, and his lips from speaking deceit."*
- Matt 12:34 *"For out of the abundance of the heart the mouth speaks."*
- Psalm 19:14 *"Let the words of my mouth and the meditation of my heart be acceptable in Your sight, O Lord, my strength and my Redeemer."*

Discussion

- Has a word ever come out of your mouth that you wish you could get back?
- How easy is it to think before you speak?
- Have you ever had anyone speak words of blessing over your life? How did it feel?
- Can we do the same for others?
- Have you ever had someone say to you, "You can do it!"? How did it change your life?
- How are your words a reflection of what is in your heart?
- Our words are important! I guess that's why the tongue gets 2 pages! ☺

A Happy Heart

Fun Fact

- The heart beats around 100,000 times per day, pumping about 2,000 gallons of blood throughout the body. If all the blood vessels in the body were laid end to end, they would stretch over 60,000 miles, enough to go around the world twice.
- Fun Fact: Octopuses have three hearts: Two hearts pump blood to their gills, while the third pumps it to the rest of their body.

Thought

- A healthy, happy & full heart is necessary for a healthy, happy & full life.

Bible

- Philippians 4:7 *"and the peace of God, which surpasses all understanding, will guard your hearts and minds through Christ Jesus."*
- Proverbs 4:23 *"Guard your heart above all else, for it determines the course of your life."*
- Acts 14:17 *"He sends you rain and good crops and gives you food and joyful hearts."*
- Proverbs 17:22 *"A cheerful heart is good medicine."*
- John 10:10 *"I have come that they may have life and have it to the full."*

Discussion

- In what ways can you guard your heart?
- Is your heart happy?
- In what ways does Jesus bring joy to your heart?
- What does it mean to fully live?
- What does it mean to live fully?

Miraculous Memory

Fun Fact

- The brain's storage capacity is believed to be equivalent to around 2.5 petabytes, enough to store 3 million hours of television.

Thought

- God never runs out of memory; He is always faithful.
- We can only remember what we have put into our brain's storage.

Bible

- Genesis 9:15 *"and I will remember my covenant with you and with all living creatures. Never again will the floodwaters destroy all life."*
- Deuteronomy 4:39 *"So remember this and keep it firmly in mind: The Lord is God both in heaven and on earth, and there is no other."*
- Deuteronomy 8:18 *"Remember the Lord your God."*
- I Chronicles 16:12 *"Remember the wonders he has performed, his miracles, and the rulings he has given,"*
- Psalm 25:6 *"Remember, O Lord, your compassion and unfailing love, which you have shown from long ages past."*
- Psalm 136:23 *"He remembered us in our weakness. His faithful love endures forever."*

Discussion

- Think about what you fill your brain's storage with.
- Do you have some memories you wish you didn't have? Ask God to heal them. He can!
- Share a time when God has remembered you.

Elephant Circles

Fun Fact

- In the wild, female elephants are known as fierce protectors. When a "sister" is giving birth, is suffering, or is in danger from an enemy, the others circle up around her, facing outward for protection.

Thought

- A circle of support is vital when going through life's journey.

Bible

- Galatians 6:2 *"Bear one another's burdens and so fulfill the law of Christ."*
- Ephesians 4:2 *"With all lowliness and gentleness, with longsuffering, bearing with one another in love,"*
- John 13:34-35 *"A new commandment I give to you, that you love one another; as I have loved you, that you also love one another. By this, all will know that you are My disciples if you have love for one another."*
- Romans 12:10 *"Be kindly affectionate to one another with brotherly love, in honor giving preference to one another."*
- Proverbs 17:17 *"A friend loves at all times."*

Discussion

- How can you be a support to someone?
- Is it easy to support someone who is suffering? Why?
- What does that look like, practically?

Moving Forward

Fun Fact

- Kangaroos can't move backward.
- Hummingbirds are the only birds that can fly backward.

Thought

- Have you ever felt stuck, or don't know which way to go? Go forward!

Bible

- Philippians 3:12-14 *"Not that I have already attained, or am already perfected; but I press on, that I may lay hold of that for which Christ Jesus has also laid hold of me. Brethren, I do not count myself to have apprehended; but one thing I do, forgetting those things which are behind and reaching forward to those things which are ahead,* [14] *I press toward the goal for the prize of the upward call of God in Christ Jesus."*

- Exodus 14:15 *"And the Lord said to Moses, 'Why do you cry to Me?' Tell the children of Israel to go forward."*

Discussion

- In what areas of your life do you feel stuck?
- Remind yourself of your goals and purpose.
- What are some practical ways to move toward those goals?

Brain Power

Fun Fact

- The brain can generate enough electricity to power a light bulb.
- The brain generates more electrical impulses in a day than all the telephones in the world combined.

Thought

- Thoughts are powerful, and what you think about the most will direct the course of your life.

Bible

- 2 Corinthians 10:5 *"We demolish arguments and every pretension that sets itself up against the knowledge of God, and we take captive every thought to make it obedient to Christ.*
- Philippians 4:6 *"Be anxious for nothing, but in everything by prayer and supplication, with thanksgiving, let your requests be made known to God."*
- Proverbs 23:7 *"For as he thinks in his heart, so is he."*

Discussion

- What do you do when so many thoughts bombard you?
- How do you handle conflicting thoughts?
- Do you have trouble with anxiety? How do you walk that out?

So Much Skin

Fun Fact

- The skin, the body's largest organ, weighs around 8 pounds and acts as a barrier against harmful microbes.
- Elephants' skin can weigh up to 2000 pounds. It can be up to 1.5 inches thick in places, providing protection and comfort.

Thought

- As skin surrounds and protects us, we can live under the shelter and protection of the Lord. He is our preeminent protector.

Bible

- Psalm 91:1-6 *Those who live in the shelter of the Most High will find rest in the shadow of the Almighty.[2] This I declare about the Lord: He alone is my refuge, my place of safety; he is my God, and I trust him.[3] For he will rescue you from every trap and protect you from deadly disease.[4] He will cover you with his feathers. He will shelter you with his wings. His faithful promises are your armor and protection....[6] Do not dread the disease that stalks in darkness, nor the disaster that strikes at midday.*

- Psalm 23:1,4 *"The Lord is my shepherd; I have all that I need.... Even when I walk through the darkest valley, I will not be afraid, for you are close beside me. Your rod and your staff protect and comfort me."*

Discussion

- What does it mean to live under the shelter of the Lord?
- Share a time when you felt protected by the Lord.

Banana Trees?

Fun Fact

- Despite their tree-like appearance, banana plants are technically giant herbs, not trees.

Thought

- Appearances can fool you. Don't judge people too quickly. Try to see them through God's eyes.

Bible

- I Samuel 16:7 "The Lord doesn't see things the way you see them. People judge by outward appearance, but the Lord looks at the heart."

- John 4:27-30 Just then his disciples came back. They were shocked to find him talking to a woman, but none of them had the nerve to ask, "What do you want with her?" or "Why are you talking to her?" [28] The woman left her water jar beside the well and ran back to the village, telling everyone, [29] "Come and see a man who told me everything I ever did! Could he possibly be the Messiah?" [30] So the people came streaming from the village to see him.

Discussion

- How quickly do you form an opinion about someone, only to find out later that you were wrong?

- Have you ever heard the phrase, "We have to keep up our appearances?" What does that mean?

- Does your outside match up with your inside? Or better yet, does your inside match up with your outside?

Sleeping Sea Otters

Fun Fact

- While floating in the water, Sea Otters sleep on their backs, holding hands! This keeps them close and from drifting apart.

Thought

- We can rest and trust the Lord, for His care is never-ending as He watches over us.

Bible

- Psalm 4:8 *"I will lie down in peace and sleep; For You alone, O Lord, make me dwell in safety."*
- Psalm 121:4 *"He will never let me stumble, slip, or fall, For He is always watching, never sleeping."*
- Proverbs 3:24 *"When you lie down, you will not be afraid, Yes, you will lie down and your sleep will be sweet."*
- Psalm 84:4 *"Better is one day in your courts than a thousand elsewhere."*

Discussion

- Do you have trouble sleeping? Thinking anxious thoughts?
- Are you fearful? Do you know that the best place to find safety and peace is close to the Lord?
- What does it mean to you to be close to the Lord?
- How can you draw closer to Him?

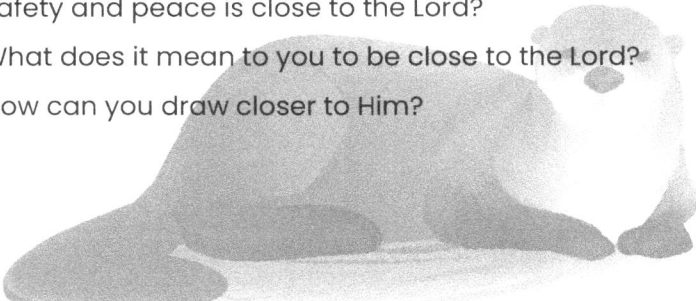

Big Bonafide Bones

Fun Fact

- Bones are vital to our health and movement. The human body has 206 bones. The longest & hardest bone in the human body is the femur, designed to support daily activities like walking and running.

Thought

- Just as we need our bones to be strong and healthy, our walk with the Lord requires strengthening daily so that we can accomplish all that He has for us.

Bible

- Proverbs 3:7,8: " *Fear the Lord and depart from evil. It will be health to your flesh and strength to your bones."*
- Proverbs 15:30 *"The light of the eyes rejoices the heart, and a good report makes the bones healthy."*
- Proverbs 16:24 *"Pleasant words are like a honeycomb, sweetness to the soul and health to the bones."*
- Isaiah 58:11 *"The Lord will guide you continually and satisfy your soul in drought and strengthen your bones. You shall be like a watered garden and like a spring of water, whose waters do not fail."*
- Ezekiel 37:4,5 *"'Prophesy to these bones and say to them,' O dry bones, hear the word of the Lord'. Thus says the Lord God to these bones,' Surely I will cause breath to enter you and you shall live.'".*

Discussion

- According to the Bible, how important are words to healthy bones?
- What areas in your life need strengthening to enable you to keep walking with the Lord?

Clamorous Cats & Birds

Fun Fact

- Cats can make more than 100 vocalizations.
- The Brown thrasher (bird) can sing up to 2000 different song types.

Thought

- Let's use our voices to praise the Lord!

Bible

- Psalm 150:6: *"Let everything that has breath praise the Lord! Praise the Lord!*
- Psalm 145:2 *"Every day I will bless You and I will praise Your name forever and ever."*
- Psalm 113:3 *"From the rising of the sun to its going down, the Lord's name is to be praised."*
- Psalm 146:1 *"Praise the Lord! Praise the Lord, O my soul! While I live, I will praise the Lord; I will sing praises to my God while I have my being."*
- Psalm 96:1 *"O sing to the Lord a new song! Sing to the Lord, all the earth!"*

Discussion

- What is your favorite worship song?
- What happens in your heart when you praise the Lord?
- What does it mean to you to sing a new song to the Lord?

Accommodating Alligators

Fun Fact

- Alligators will give manatees the right of way if they are swimming near each other.

Thought

- Preferring others is a character trait to be practiced.

Bible

- Philippians 2:3,4 *"Let nothing be done through selfish ambition or conceit, but in lowliness of mind let each esteem others better than himself. Let each of you look out not only for his own interests, but also for the interests of others."*

- Luke 6:31 *"And just as you want men to do to you, you also do to them likewise."*

Discussion

- How hard is it for you to prefer others?
- What does it look like to make room for others?
- Do you ever find yourself rolling your eyes at someone?
- Do you think too highly of yourself?

Tasty Tips

Fun Fact

- Butterflies can taste with their feet to help them determine if a leaf is a suitable source to lay their eggs.
- Fish have taste buds all over their bodies, including their skin and fins.
- Humans have approximately 9,000 taste buds and cows can have up to 25,000 taste buds.

Thought

- You may be the only tangible expression of Jesus that people ever see. When people interact with us, do they get a taste of the sweetness of Jesus?

Bible

- Psalm 34:8 *"O taste and see that the Lord is good; Blessed is the man who trusts in Him!"*
- Psalm 119:103 *"How sweet are Your words to my taste, sweeter than honey to my mouth."*
- 2 Corinthians 2:15 *"For we are a fragrance of Christ to God among those who are being saved and among those who are perishing."*

Discussion

- How can you be the sweetness of Jesus to others?
- Are your words sweet? Is your attitude sweet? Are your actions sweet?

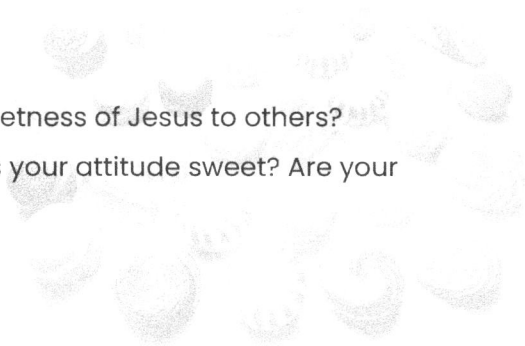

Long and Strong

Fun Fact

- The longest English word is 189,819 letters long. (It's the chemical name for the largest known protein, titin.) It would be too long to write here. ☺ -------------------->
- Psalm 119 is the longest chapter in the Bible.

Thought

- Life is not a sprint, it's a marathon! Let your walk with Jesus be long and strong!

Bible

- Hebrews 12:2 *"Looking unto Jesus, the author and finisher of our faith."*
- Jude 1:21 *"Keep yourselves in the love of God, looking for the mercy of our Lord Jesus Christ unto eternal life."*
- Philippians 3:12 *"Not that I have already attained, or am already perfected; but I press on, that I may lay hold of that for which Christ Jesus has also laid hold of me."*

Discussion

- Are there life challenges you are facing that make you want to give up? Are you discouraged in your walk with Jesus?
- What are some ways you can encourage yourself in the Lord?
- A marathon runner takes one step at a time. What does that mean to you?

Stubborn Sheep

Fun Fact

- When sheep graze, their neck and shoulder muscles engage, making it nearly impossible to move them. And sheep are insatiably hungry, grazing whenever possible. To move the sheep, a shepherd uses the crook of his staff to lift their heads, releasing those muscles, allowing them to move freely.

Thought

- Sometimes, like sheep, we focus on one thing and get stubborn. We need the gentle touch of our Good Shepherd to help us look up, see Him, and stay flexible.

Bible

- Psalm 78:8 "...A stubborn and rebellious generation. A generation that did not set its heart a right, and whose spirit was not faithful to God."
- Psalm 121:1,2 "I will lift up my eyes to the hills– from where comes my help? My help comes from the Lord who made heaven and earth."
- Proverbs 16:9 "A man's heart plans his way, but the Lord directs his steps."

Discussion

- Do you find yourself being stubborn and unmovable?
- Do you argue with others a lot?
- What does it mean to surrender to the Lord?
- How can you stay flexible with your opinions?

Terrific Tigers

Fun Fact

- Tigers have striped skin, not just fur. The stripes are like fingerprints- no two tigers have the same pattern. Tigers are the largest of the wild cats, and Bengal Tigers can be up to 10 feet long!

Thought

- Our terrific-ness comes from our identity in Christ. God fashioned each one of us for His mission and purpose for our lives. Our joy is found in knowing Jesus and allowing Him to be displayed in our lives.

Bible

- Philippians 1:21 *"For to me, to live is Christ, and to die is gain. Jesus, the author and finisher of our faith."*
- Galatians 2:20 *"I have been crucified with Christ; it is no longer I who live, but Christ lives in me; and the life which I now live in the flesh I live by faith in the Son of God, who loved me and gave Himself for me."*
- Colossians 1:27 *"Christ in you, the hope of glory."*
- Isaiah 43:10 *"You are My witnesses, says the Lord, And My servant whom I have chosen, that you may know and believe Me, and understand that I am He. Before Me there was no God formed, nor shall there be after Me."*

Discussion

- Do you know God has a purpose and mission for your life?
- Have you ever thought about the way God designed you to fulfill this purpose?
- Is it possible to accomplish this without Jesus? Or without knowing our identity in Him?
- How do we display Christ?

Sonic Sneezes

Fun Fact

- A sneeze can travel at speeds of up to 100 miles an hour, spreading around 100,000 germs into the air. The spray can travel anywhere from a 5 to 30-foot radius from where you sneezed, and sneezing is impossible while sleeping.

Thought

- Spread the good news about Jesus and His never-ending love!

Bible

- Matthew 9:31 *"When they had departed, they spread the news about Him in all that country."* (2 Blind men healed by Jesus)
- Mark 1:28 *"And immediately His fame spread throughout all the region around Galilee."*
- Acts 13:49 *"And the Word of the Lord was being spread throughout all the region."*
- Acts 1:8 *"But you shall receive power when the Holy Spirit has come upon you; and you shall be witnesses to Me in Jerusalem, and in all Judea and Samaria, and to the end of the earth."*

Discussion

- Allodoxaphobia is the fear of other people's opinions. Do people's opinions stop you from spreading the Good News of Jesus?
- Just as the blind men had a reason to spread the news, Do you have a reason to? What is it?
- How does the Holy Spirit empower us to be His witnesses?
- Do you need a fresh touch from the Holy Spirit to spark some boldness for spreading the Gospel? Just ask Him!

Concluding Considerations

Bible

- Jeremiah 33:3 *"Call to Me, and I will answer you, and show you great and mighty things, which you do not know."*

Thought

- Our infinite, all-knowing, all-powerful, ever-present God invites and welcomes us to know Him. This statement, in and of itself, is mind-boggling to me! Yet true!
- He has all wisdom and invites us to seek Him, promising to give us His mind and thoughts.
- He has displayed His magnificence throughout creation and given us 5 senses to discover this.

Most Important Thought

- Most importantly, He invites us into a personal relationship with Him, through His Son, Jesus Christ. He's saying, 'There's more room in the family of God, and you're invited!"
- He loves and accepts you completely, just the way you are! God doesn't make you work for something Jesus has already paid for... our salvation!
- All you need to do is accept His invitation today, and your life will never be the same. He has an amazing adventure waiting for you!

Bible

- John 3:16 *"For God so loved the world that He gave His one and only Son, that whoever believes in Him shall not perish but have eternal life."*

- Romans 10:9 *"If you confess with your mouth the Lord Jesus Christ and believe in your heart that God has raised Him from the dead, you will be saved."*

- John 14:1,10 *"Let not your heart be troubled, you believe in God, believe also in Me...Jesus said to him, "I am the way, the truth and the life. No one comes to the Father except through Me."*

- John 1:12 *"But as many as received Him, to them He gave the right to become children of God, to those who believe in His name."*

- John 10:10 *"I have come that they may have life, and that they may have it more abundantly."*

* If you accept His invitation today, please write me so I can celebrate with you!   joanewood@gmail.com

Thought

- If you've accepted Jesus as your Lord and Savior, but feel stuck, Jesus sent the Holy Spirit to empower us to live supernaturally abundant lives.

- The Holy Spirit is a gift, not a reward. Just receive Him as you've already received Jesus.

- The same Spirit that raised Christ from the dead lives in you and empowers us to live with a new purpose...His witnesses!

- As we stay close to Jesus, stay connected to Him, we produce the fruit of the Holy Spirit: love, joy, peace, patience and more.

- We can live in the resurrection power of the Holy Spirit every day. We are filled, sent, and unstoppable carriers of the Gospel.

Bible

- Galatians 2:22,23 *"But the fruit of the Spirit is love, joy, peace, patience, kindness, goodness, faithfulness, gentleness & self-control."*

- Acts 1:8 *"But you shall receive power when the Holy Spirit has come upon you; and you shall be witnesses to Me in Jerusalem, and in all Judea and Samaria, and to the end of the earth."*

- Acts 15:32 *"And the disciples were filled with joy and with the Holy Spirit."*

- Romans 15:13 *"Now may the God of hope fill you with all joy and peace in believing, that you may abound in hope by the power of the Holy Spirit."*

Bonus Fun Facts

- One strand of spaghetti is called a "spaghetto."
- The longest hiccup in history lasted for more than 60 years after it began.
- A shrimp's heart is in its head.
- It is physically impossible for pigs to look up into the sky.
- The "sixth sick sheik's sixth sheep's sick" is believed to be the toughest tongue twister in the English language.
- Portions of the Bible have been translated into 3,300 languages. Among those include fictional languages, like Elvish and Klingon.

joanewood@gmail.com

www.ingramcontent.com/pod-product-compliance
Lightning Source LLC
Chambersburg PA
CBHW040825040426
42339CB00017B/484